1910: Manufacture of Bakelite begins plastic age.

1962: Marion Stoddart organizes the Nashua River Cleanup Committee, and the city of Leominster gets permission from the Massachusetts Department of Public Health to dump 150 million gallons of raw sewage per day into the Nashua.

1965: U.S. Congress passes Clean Water Act. Paper companies along the Nashua join together to build a treatment plant, and 400–500 youths work for five months to clear trash from Nashua's riverbed and banks.

1970: U.S. Environmental Protection Agency (EPA) formed, and Federal Clean Water Act states that all U.S. waters be fishable and swimmable by 1983.

1979: Bass, pickerel, perch, trout, bald eagles, osprey, and great blue heron return to the Nashua.

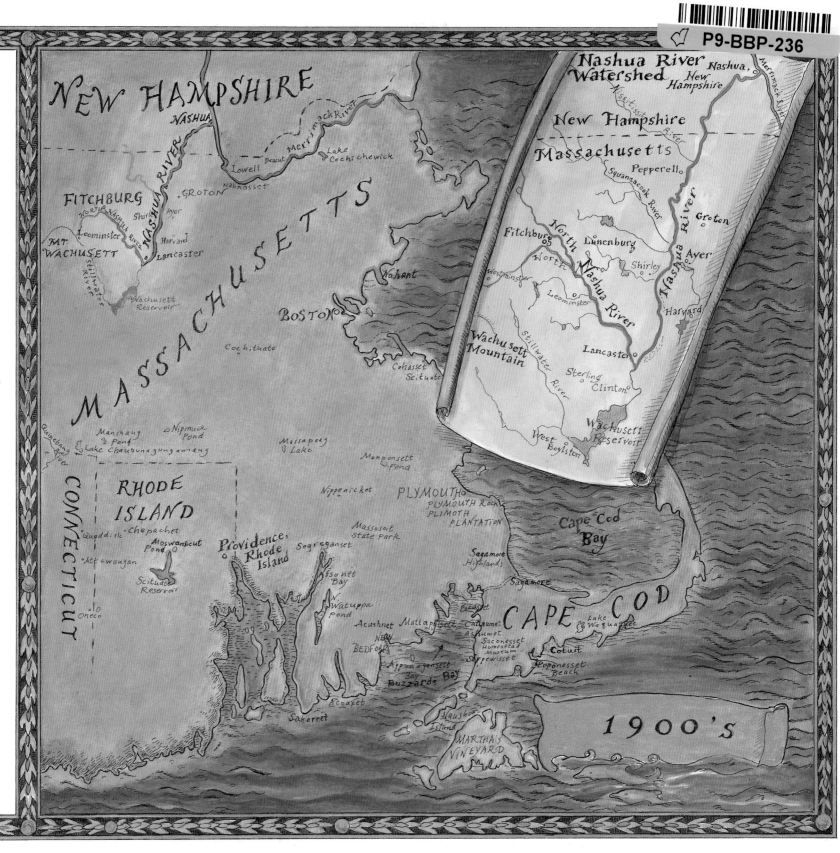

The Nashua River Valley 1400 - 1990

A RIVER RAN WILD

AN ENVIRONMENTAL HISTORY

Lynne Cherry

A Gulliver Green Book
Harcourt Brace & Company
SAN DIEGO   NEW YORK   LONDON

Requests for permission to make copies of
any part of the work should be mailed to
Permissions Department,
Harcourt Brace & Company,
8th Floor, Orlando, Florida 32887.

The area of the Nashua that I have written about covers approximately 60 miles.
It would have been impossible to illustrate the entire length affected
by the river cleanup in this story. Most of the polluting mills were in Fitchburg,
but I have portrayed a more pastoral part of the Nashua for artistic purposes
and also because Marion Stoddart makes her home in the Ayer-Groton area.
This area of New England has maintained its colonial character
and, in places, has changed little from colonial days.

Library of Congress Cataloging-in-Publication Data
Cherry, Lynne.
A river ran wild/by Lynne Cherry. —1st ed.
p.   cm.
"Gulliver books."
Summary: An environmental history of the Nashua River,
from its discovery by Indians
through the polluting years of the Industrial Revolution
to the ambitious cleanup that revitalized it.
ISBN 0-15-200542-0
1. Nashua River (Mass. and N.H.) —History —Juvenile literature.
2. Nashua River Valley (Mass. and N.H.) —History —Juvenile literature.
3. Water quality —Nashua River (Mass. and N.H.) —History —Juvenile literature.
4. Man —Influence on nature —Nashua River (Mass. and N.H.) —History —Juvenile literature.
5. Indians of North America —Nashua River (Mass. and N.H.) —History —Juvenile literature.
[1. Nashua River (Mass. and N.H.) —History.
2. Man —Influence on nature.]
I. Title.
F72.N37044   1992
974.4′ —dc20   91-12892

C D E F G

Printed in Singapore

The illustrations in this book were done in watercolors,
colored pencils, and Dr. Martin's watercolors on
Strathmore 400 watercolor paper.
Composition by Thompson Type, San Diego, California
Color separations were made by Bright Arts, Ltd., Singapore.
Printed and bound by Tien Wah Press, Singapore
Production supervision by Warren Wallerstein and Ginger Boyer
Designed by Michael Farmer

*To my husband, Eric Fersht, who has
devoted his life to protecting the environment*

AUTHOR'S NOTE

THIS STORY ABOUT THE NASHUA RIVER is true. As early as seven thousand years ago, Indian peoples came through the Nashua River Valley. They hunted animals and gathered seeds and plants to eat. When these Algonquin-speaking Indian people settled by the Nashua River, they combined planting food crops with hunting, gathering, and fishing. The crops were planted along the river on what are called flood plains, where, every spring, the floodwaters (called freshets) deposited silt on the banks, making the ground very fertile. The Nashua hunted in the uplands and streams.

The English who arrived in the Nashua Valley in the 1600s came with a different philosophy toward nature than the Indians had. In England they had believed that the forests were full of evil spirits and they brought these views with them to America. At first the Indians were friendly, but as the colonists began to claim Indian hunting and fishing land as their own, the Indians began to fight to preserve their way of life.

In the mid-1700s dams were built on the Nashua, and gristmills and sawmills used the Nashua's water power to operate. Textile and paper factories were built in the 1800s. During these years, the river was also used for swimming and fishing. But, by the 1960s, the Nashua River was so clogged with waste that it was declared ecologically dead.

Much of the pollution originated from mills in Fitchburg, Mass., which was a developed city by the early 1900s. The pollution was carried downstream through smaller Massachusetts towns such as Ayer, Pepperell, and Groton. When Marion Stoddart moved to Groton in 1962, she set out to establish a greenway (trees running the length of the river on both sides) along the Nashua. But the state of Massachusetts wasn't interested in buying land along such a filthy river. So Marion organized the Nashua River Cleanup Committee. When she and her supporters spoke to state officials, they were told that there were no laws to keep mills and factories from dumping chemicals, dyes, and waste into the river. In response, the Nashua River Cleanup Committee began their campaign to have laws created. They presented bottles of dirty Nashua River water to politicians. They asked businessmen to help convince the paper companies to build a treatment plant. They cleaned away garbage from the Nashua's banks. They spoke at town meetings. And they began to lobby for laws to protect all rivers.

In 1965 the U.S. Congress passed the first Clean Water Act. The next year, Marion Stoddart coordinated a successful citizen campaign that led to the passage of the Massachusetts Clean Water Act of 1966. In December 1970 the National Environmental Protection Agency was established. In 1969 Marion Stoddart's group renamed itself the Nashua River Watershed Association and began working on protecting the small rivers which run into the Nashua, and providing a greenway along the banks of the Nashua and its tributaries.

In this book, the Indian Oweana's dream is an allegory for his and Marion's vision. Even when the river was filthy, Marion and other people had a vision of what the river would look like clean. This vision of an unpolluted earth continues to drive people today to work to clean up their environment. John Berger begins his book *Restoring the Earth* with these words: "Imagine a world where the rivers and streams flow clean again, brilliant and teeming with fish. The air is fresh and crystalline. The earth, once bare and robbed of its topsoil, now is green with healthy vegetation. This vision of Nature thriving and restored can become reality." This book is about how one woman's vision and determination changed the face and the future of the Nashua River. I hope that this story inspires its readers to be people who try to make a difference in the world.

— LYNNE CHERRY

LONG AGO a river ran wild through a land of towering forests. Bears, moose, and herds of deer, hawks and owls all made their homes in the peaceful river valley. Geese paused on their long migration and rested on its banks. Beavers, turtles, and schools of fish swam in its clear waters.

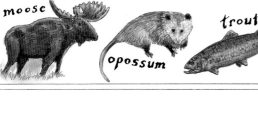

One day a group of native people, searching for a place to settle, came upon the river valley. From atop the highest mountain, known today as Mt. Wachusett, they saw the river nestled in its valley, a silver sliver in the sun.

They came down from the mountain, and at the river's edge they knelt to quench their thirst with its clear water. Pebbles shone up from the bottom.

"Let us settle by this river," said the chief of the native people. He named the river Nash-a-way — River with the Pebbled Bottom.

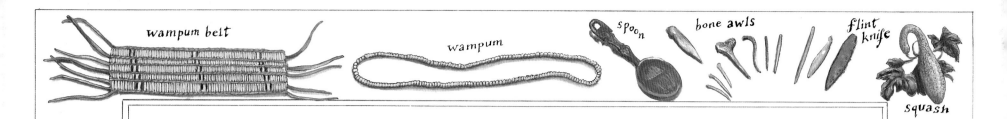

wampum belt · *wampum* · *spoon* · *bone awls* · *flint knife*

squash

woven baskets

zucchini

woven baskets

clay pipes

pestle

purse

comb

clay pipes

clay pots

By the Nash-a-way, Chief Weeawa's people built a village. They gathered cattails from the riverbanks to thatch their dwellings. In the forest they set fires to clear brush from the forest floor. In these clearings they planted corn and squash for eating. They made arrows for hunting and canoes for river travel.

When the Indians hunted in the forest or caught salmon in the river, they killed only what they needed for themselves for food and clothing. They asked all the forest creatures that they killed to please forgive them.

The Nashua people saw a rhythm in their lives and in the seasons. The river, land, and forest provided all they needed.

mortar · *arrowheads* · *quiver and bow* · *stone ax* · *antler flaking tools* · *wooden bowl*

shell hoe · *arrow* · *stone hoe*

The Nashua had lived for generations by the clear, clean, flowing river when one day a pale-skinned trader came with a boatload full of treasures. He brought shiny metal knives, colored beads, and cooking kettles, mirrors, tools, and bolts of bright cloth. His wares seemed like magic. The Nashua welcomed him, traded furs, and soon a trading post was built.

Surrounding the text, illustrated border labels read (clockwise from top-left): rake, razorback hog, trivets, hoe, spinning, sheep, turkey, well bucket, spinning wheel, cider press, spinning wheel, goose, spinning jenny, metal spoon, horse, plow, wagon, rooster, butter churn, guinea hen, candlemaking, fireplace implements.

In the many years that followed, the settlers' village and others like it grew and the Nash-a-way became the Nashua. The settlers worked together to clear land by cutting down the forests, which they thought were full of danger — wilderness that they would conquer. They hunted wolves and beaver, killing much more than they needed. Extra pelts were sent to England in return for goods and money.

The settlers built sawmills along the river, which the Nashua's current powered. They built dams to make the millponds that were used to store the water. They cut down the towering forest and floated tree trunks down the river. The logs were cut up into lumber, which was used for building houses.

The settlers built fences for their pastures, plowed the fields, and planted crops. They called the land their own and told the Indians not to trespass. Hunting land disappeared as the settlers cleared the forest. Indian fishing rights vanished as the settlers claimed the river.

The Indians' ways were disrupted and they began to fight the settlers. The wars raged for many years but the Indians' bows and arrows were no match against gunpowder, and so the settlers' rifles drove the Indians from the land.

Through a hundred years of fighting, the Nashua was a healthy river, sometimes dammed for grist and sawmills, but still flowing wild and free. Muskrats, fish, and turtles still swam from bank to bank. Deer still came to drink from the river, and owls, raccoons, and beaver fed there.

first sewing machine

Civil War

loom

Shortest and Most Direct Route From Points in New England "FIVE EXPRESS TRAINS LEAVE ALBANY DAILY"

Main St. Bridge Nashua, New Hampshire

mill

first telephone

Edison electric light invented

camera invented 1839

clock

typewriter invented

bicycle invented

young factory workers

Crompton Loom 1876

Edison phonograph

At the start of the new century, an industrial revolution came to the Nashua's banks and waters. Many new machines were invented. Some spun thread from wool and cotton. Others wove the thread into cloth. Some machines turned wood to pulp, and others made the pulp into paper. Leftover pulp and dye and fiber was dumped into the Nashua River, whose swiftly flowing current washed away the waste.

canal at West Boylston

old bridge in Boylston

Junction of Nashua and Merrimack Rivers

1882 first Bell telephone

wool card

mill at South Lancaster

These were times of much excitement, times of "progress" and "invention." Factories along the Nashua River made new things of new materials. Telephones and radios and other things were made of plastics. Chemicals and plastic waste were also dumped into the river. Soon the Nashua's fish and wildlife grew sick from this pollution.

The paper mills continued to pollute the Nashua's waters. Every day for many decades pulp was dumped into the Nashua, and as the pulp clogged up the river, it began to run more slowly.

As the pulp decomposed, bad smells welled up from the river. People who lived near the river smelled its stench and stayed far from it. Each day as the mills dyed paper red, green, blue, and yellow, the Nashua ran whatever color the paper was dyed.

Soon no fish lived in the river. No birds stopped on their migration. No one could see pebbles shining up through murky water. The Nashua was dark and dirty. The Nashua was slowly dying.

plastic appliances

fish killed by pollution

DANGER
WATER
POLLUTED
No Swimming
BOARD OF HEALTH

first human in space

pollution

nuclear power

electric car

electric typewriter

electric clock of the 60's

pollution

pollution

Earth from space 1970 - first Earth Day

traffic jam

1969 plastic water jug

LAOS Vietnam War VIETNAM THAILAND CAMBODIA

One night Oweana, a descendant of Weeawa who still lived by the Nashua, had a dream so vivid that he awoke in wide-eyed wonder. In his dream Chief Weeawa's spirit returned to the river and saw it as it was now — still and deadly.

Chief Weeawa mourned for the Nash-a-way, but where his tears fell upon the dirty waters, the waters were cleansed until the river once again flowed freely.

The next morning Oweana went to speak to his friend Marion. When he told her of his dream, she said, "I had this dream also! River with the Pebbled Bottom is the name Weeawa gave it, but today no pebbles shine up through the Nashua River's waters." Together they decided something must be done.

Drive For Nashua River Cleanup Moves Ahead
More Than 800 Sign Groton Petition

HOLD YOUR NOSE! NASHUA RIVER AHEAD!

Gov. Receives Sample of River Water
Petitions With 6,287 Names Presented To Gov. Volpe

Senator Kennedy Views Nashua River

Collecting water sample

STOP POLLUTING NASHUA

Marion Stoddart

NASHUA RIVER WATERSHED ASSOCIATION

Marion traveled to each town along the Nashua. She spoke of the river's history and of her vision to restore it. "No longer do we have a river — it's a stinking, smelly sewer. But it wasn't always this way."

People listened and imagined a sparkling river, full of fish. They imagined pebbles shining up through clear waters. They signed petitions and sent letters. They protested to politicians and showed them jars of dirty water. They convinced the paper mills to build a plant to process the waste. They persuaded the factories to stop dumping. Finally, new laws were passed and the factories stopped polluting.

GROTON

LANCASTER

Udall Calls Clean Water Drive An Economic Necessity For Area

Thank You, Gentlemen

FITCHBURG SENTINEL 3/16/69
Historic Action: Nashua Cleanup Funds Approved

Slowly, slowly, the Nashua's current began to clean its water. Year by year the river carried away the dyes and fiber to the ocean. Marion and Oweana thanked the people who had helped to clean the Nashua.

Through the meadows, towns, and cities, the Nashua once again flows freely. Paper pulp no longer clogs it. Chemicals no longer foul it.

Now we walk along its banks and row upon its fragrant waters. We can set our boats upon it and with its current, drift downstream.

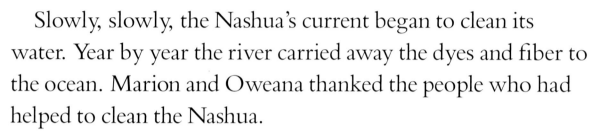

Once again the river runs wild through a towering forest greenway. Red-tailed hawks and barred owls live here. Geese pause from their long migration and rest on the riverbanks. Deer come to drink from the river's waters. We, too, have settled by this river. Pebbles shine up through clear water. Nashua is what we call it — River with the Pebbled Bottom.

ACKNOWLEDGMENTS

I OWE SPECIAL THANKS to the two people who inspired this book: Professor William Cronon and his book *Changes in the Land* (Hill & Wang, 1983) and Professor John J. Berger and his book *Restoring the Earth* (Knopf, 1985; Doubleday Anchor, 1987). William Cronon's book provided the philosophical underpinnings for *A River Ran Wild*. In his book he documents the different philosophies that the Indians and the settlers had toward the land and how, ultimately, the settlers' view of nature as a collection of commodities led to the environmental degradation I write about in my book. John Berger's book documents twelve environmental success stories of individuals who have, through their vision and dedication, changed their world for the better. Marion Stoddart is one of these individuals. I owe a special thanks to Marion. John Berger's story of Marion's cleanup of the Nashua inspired *A River Ran Wild*. Marion herself read and reread my manuscript, studied my illustrations for accuracy, clarified many times how the battle to clean up the Nashua was fought, took me for canoe trips on the Nashua, and drove me around Ayer and Groton, Mass., so I could photograph the mills and the river. I am deeply indebted to her for all her help, and I can only hope that when I am 63, I am still as visionary, caring, youthful, and spry as she is.

Thanks also to Bonnie Bick of the National Colonial Farm in Accokeek, Md.; Trudie Lamb Richmond at the American Indian Archeological Institute, Washington, Conn.; Erin and Winnea Lamb (Wunneanatsu), American Indians for Development, Meriden, Conn.; Larry Anderson, Little Compton, R.I.; Mel Coombs, Cotuit, Mass.; Onk Wetase (Edward J. Guillemette), Dracut, Mass., who is the model for Chief Weeawa; Maggie Stier, Fruitlands Museum, Harvard, Mass.; Shelly Finn and Ed Himlin of the Nashua River Watershed Assoc., Fitchburg, Mass.; Old Sturbridge Village, Mass., and Tom Kelleher, in particular; Professor Bill Stapp, U. Michigan, Ann Arbor, Mich.; The Museum of American Textile History, N. Andover, Mass.; Plimoth Plantation, Plymouth, Mass.; Fitchburg Historical Society, Fitchburg, Mass.; and Bob Karalus, Indian expert, for sharing his knowledge.

A special thanks to the Smithsonian Environmental Research Center (SERC) in Edgewater, Md., for providing me with an artist-in-residency and especially to Mark Haddon, Director of Public Programs, and David Correll, Director of SERC.

Thanks to Rubin Pfeffer and Liz Van Doren at HBJ: to Rubin for seeing the importance of publishing such books as this and to Liz for being such an excellent editor.

7000 years ago: Indian peoples come through the Nashua River Valley.

1400: Nashua Indian people of the Pennacook Confederacy settle along the Nashua River.

1600s: First colonial settlements in New England

1616–17: Indian settlements devastated by smallpox epidemic

1628: Massachusetts Bay Colony founded

1675–76: King Philip's (Metacomet) War

1776: Declaration of Independence

1830: Indian Removal Act

1848–60: Wave of immigrants come from Europe, many work in factories.

1850: Paper manufacture, textiles, and shoe products become the prevalent industries on the river.

1899: Largest dam on the Nashua River—the Wachusett Dam in Clinton—built to provide Boston with water.